AF261452

GOOD PRINTED THINGS

A Note from the Author

The Upstate of South Carolina is a beautiful place to call home. But it's not just *our* home. A special group of plants, animals, and fungi have lived here for a very long time. These species are called natives, and many of them live in our own backyards and favorite outdoor spaces. These different species are all connected, like a giant web, and they work together to support each other. Each one has an important role to play, just like you and me!

This book will introduce you to 26 native wild things of the Upstate. Learning about these unique species—their habitats, relationships, and how to care for them—is one way you can be a part of making our Upstate home a beautiful, safe place for everyone, and every*thing*.

— Abby

Written by Abby Moore Keith
Illustrated by Carissa Grace Bowser
Book Design by Lib Ramos

Copyright © 2024 Good Printed Things. All rights reserved.

No part of this book may be reproduced without written permission of the publisher.
For permission or to order books in bulk for educational use, email contact@goodprintedthings.com.

Printed in The United States of America
First Edition, Second Printing
ISBN: 978-1-7345844-8-6

goodprintedthings.com

A is for American toad

Anaxyrus americanus

B is for Brook trout
Salvelinus fontinalis

I'm a freshwater fish that's
speckled and green.

I like mountain creeks
where the water is clean.

C is for Carolina wren

Thryothorus ludovicianus

I may be small, but my song is mighty.
Look for my nest. It's a bit untidy.

D is for Dogwood
Cornus florida

I grow in the woods under tall canopies.
My flowers make food for small native bees.

E is for Ebony jewelwing damselfly
Calopteryx maculata

My body is green and my wings are black.
Mosquito larva is my favorite snack.

F is for Five-lined skink
Plestiodon fasciatus

G is for Goldenrod
Solidago altissima

H is for Hearts-a-bustin'
Euonymus americanus

My fruit is red, but I'm no strawberry.
The deer love me, but humans—be wary!

I is for Indigo bunting
Passerina cyanea

When we migrate
through the night,

we use the stars to
guide our flight.

J is for Jewelweed
Impatiens capensis

K is for ruby-crowned Kinglet

Corthylio calendula

I'm a tough little bird
with a bright red crest,

which is plain to see
when I defend my nest.

L is for Little brown bat
Myotis lucifugus

At dusk I catch mosquitoes with ease.
Build me a box. I'm an imperiled species.

M is for Milkweed tiger moth
Euchaetes egle

I'm a cute caterpillar, but I'm no treat.
My clicks tell bats I'm not good to eat.

N is for Northern watersnake
Nerodia sipedon

All is well, I'm no water moccasin.

I have round pupils and blotches on my skin.

O is for river Otter
Lontra canadensis

P is for Pink lady's slipper

Cypripedium acaule

I trap bees
inside my funnel.

They pollinate
me through my
exit tunnel.

Q is for Quercus (KWER-kus)

Oak genus

R is for Rosebay rhododendron

Rhododendron maximum

I'm a mountain shrub. I help prevent floods.
I welcome summer with pink and white buds.

S is for Swamp rabbit
Sylvilagus aquaticus

I'm a rare breed. Some call me cane-cutter.
I live in canebrakes and thickets near water.

T is for eastern painted Turtle
Chrysemys picta

I brumate*
in water where
air's hard to find.

To get oxygen,
I use my behind.

*Brumation is when reptiles sleep during the cold winter months, like mammals hibernate.

U is for Ursus americanus
(UR-sus ah-mer-ih-KAY-nus)
American black bear

V is for arrowwood Viburnum
Viburnum dentatum

My stems are straight
and my flowers are white.

Birds find my berries
an August delight.

W is for Witches' butter
Tremella mesenterica
W
Find me on dead trees.
I'm yellow and gummy.
Turn me into candy.
I promise I'm yummy!

X is for *Xylocopa virginica*

(ZY-loh-KOH-puh ver-JIN-ih-kuh)

Eastern carpenter bee

We chew holes into wood to make our nests.
We're good pollinators, not garden pests.

Y is for Yellow-bellied sapsucker
Sphyrapicus varius

Listen in winter for
my "tap, tap, tap."

I drill holes in trees
and lick out the sap.

Z is for Zebra swallowtail butterfly
Eurytides marcellus

I lay my eggs on
pawpaw trees.

When my larvae hatch,
they eat the leaves.

Glossary

American toad
Anaxyrus americanus (ah-NAK-syoo-rus ah-mer-ih-KAY-nus)

American toads live in ponds, roadside ditches, or anywhere with wet hiding spots and plenty of insects to eat. In winter when the daylight begins to get longer, male toads let us know spring is on its way by gathering together at night and singing to the females.

Where: Backyards, parks, and wild spaces with shallow water

Brook trout
Salvelinus fontinalis (sal-vuh-LYE-nus fon-TIN-uh-lis)

Also called southern Appalachian brook trout, these rare fish are found in cool mountain streams. Brook trout are treasured for their speckled bodies and the orange and red color their bellies turn when they breed, but there aren't many left in South Carolina.

Where: Remote, clean headwater streams in the mountains

Carolina wren
Thryothorus ludovicianus (THRY-oh-THOR-us loo-doh-VIH-see-ay-nus)

The Carolina wren is our State Bird and for a good reason. It's a common backyard visitor and a cheerful singer—you'll probably hear one before you see it. Mostly the male sings, which sounds like "teakettle, teakettle," but sometimes the female will chime in with "trill, trill, trill." These birds build their nests in creative places like old pots, boots, and even windowsills.

Where: Backyards, parks, and wild spaces with food sources and trees and shrubs for cover

Dogwood
Cornus florida (KOR-nus FLOR-ih-duh)

The dogwood is a small tree found in backyards and wooded areas. In spring its branches are covered with white petals, or bracts, grouped in fours. Dogwood pollen is an important food source for special native bees and the leaves feed the spring azure caterpillar. In the fall, it produces small red fruit that is packed with calcium and fat—a perfect snack for birds!

Where: Backyards, parks, and wild spaces with woodland canopies

Ebony jewelwing damselfly
Calopteryx maculata (kuh-LOP-ter-iks mak-yoo-LAH-tuh)

This beautiful bug is easy to spot because the male's metallic green body sparkles in sunlight. They like shaded streams with lots of plants where they can find mosquitoes to eat. Look for them resting in sunny spots on branches or leaves. When still, they fold their wings up like a butterfly, not a dragonfly, whose wings spread out like an airplane.

Where: Parks and wild spaces with water

Five-lined skink
Plestiodon fasciatus (PLES-tee-oh-don fas-ee-AY-tus)

These medium-sized lizards are named for the five lines running down their body—two on each side and one down the center of their back. They live in wooded areas with plenty of trees and stumps to hide in. As they age, their bright blue tails fade, but they still break them off when grabbed to distract predators and escape.

Where: Wooded areas in backyards, parks, and wild spaces

Goldenrod 🔭
Solidago altissima (sol-ih-DAY-go al-TISS-ih-muh)

This type of goldenrod, called "tall," is our State Wildflower. Look for it in fields and along roadsides, especially in early fall when its yellow flowers let us know cold weather is on the way. Goldenrod feeds butterflies, native bees, and birds, who find shelter in large fields of it. These flowers get blamed for causing allergies, but that's goldenrod's look-alike, ragweed.

Where: Backyards, parks, and wild spaces with open fields

Hearts-a-bustin' 🔭 🔭
Euonymus americanus (yoo-ON-ih-mus ah-mer-ih-KAY-nus)

Also known as a strawberry bush, this small shrub is found in wet woodlands and along creeks and rivers. Hearts-a-bustin' gets its name from the bumpy red fruits that burst open in fall to reveal bright orange seeds. If eaten in large quantities, the seeds are toxic to humans, but it's called "deer candy" for a reason. White-tailed deer will eat the entire plant down to twigs.

Where: Wooded areas in backyards, parks, and wild spaces

Indigo bunting 🔭 🔭
Passerina cyanea (pas-uh-REE-nuh sy-AN-ee-uh)

These vibrant songbirds aren't common in cities or neighborhoods. They like wide brushy pastures or old fields near trees. The females are brown, and the males are only blue during spring and summer. An easy way to remember their song is, "fire, fire, where, where, here, here." A study in the 1960s discovered that buntings use stars to navigate when they migrate.

Where: Open fields with tall grasses and trees and shrubs for cover

Jewelweed 🔭
Impatiens capensis (im-PAY-shens kuh-PEN-sis)

Keep an eye out for this fun native wildflower from midsummer to the first frost. Its small orange blooms can be found along stream banks and wet woodlands. It's called touch-me-not for a reason. When the blooms form into slender seed pods, a slight squeeze will cause the seeds to shoot out of their pods.

Where: Backyards, parks, and wild spaces with water

Kinglet, ruby-crowned 🔭 🔭
Corthylio calendula (kor-THY-lee-oh kuh-LEN-joo-luh)

Spot these feisty little birds after the first frost, when they venture down from their pine tree homes to wooded areas and backyards. With their dull yellow bodies and black-and-white-striped wings, kinglets may seem plain, but don't be fooled. When excited or angry, a ruby streak pops up on the male's tiny head, like a punk rocker with a red mohawk.

Where: Backyards, parks, and wild spaces with food sources and trees and shrubs for cover

Little brown bat 🔭 🔭 🔭
Myotis lucifugus (my-OH-tis loo-SIH-fyoo-gus)

These flying mammals can live up to 30 years and are great pest killers—they can eat 15 mosquitoes a minute! The little brown bat, along with other bat species in the Upstate, are quickly disappearing due to white-nose syndrome, a disease caused by a fungus that attacks bats during hibernation. Hanging bat boxes can help provide fungus-free homes for bats.

Where: Bat species are hard to identify. Look for different species near abandoned buildings, open fields, parks, and wild spaces at dusk.

Milkweed tiger moth 🔭 🔭
Euchaetes egle (yoo-KAY-teez EE-glee)

With gray wings and an orange abdomen, the adult milkweed tiger moth isn't very noticeable, but the caterpillar is! Covered in black, white, and orange tufts, you can find this fuzzy fellow munching on milkweed plants right alongside monarch caterpillars. Like other moths, it has a special organ that makes ultrasonic sounds to warn bats and other predators of its toxicity.

Where: Backyards, parks, and wild spaces with milkweed plants

Northern watersnake 🔭
Nerodia sipedon (neh-ROH-dee-uh sih-PEE-don)

Often mistaken for water moccasins, the northern watersnake is not venomous and is common in our lakes, ponds, and rivers where it can find plenty of fish and frogs to eat. Water moccasins have thicker bodies, narrow cat-like pupils, and don't live in the Upstate, while northern watersnakes have round pupils, rectangular blotches, and slender bodies.

Where: Backyards, parks, and wild spaces with water

Otter, river 🔭 🔭 🔭
Lontra canadensis (LON-truh kan-uh-DEN-sis)

North American river otters can be hard to find. They like to live away from humans, and are often found along lakes and river banks—even in abandoned beaver lodges. Like many species, otters benefit from the wetland habitats beavers create by building dams. Otters are playful and curious, and they like to eat fish, frogs, and crawfish.

Where: Remote areas in parks and wild spaces with water

Pink lady's slipper 🔭 🔭 🔭
Cypripedium acaule (sy-prih-PEE-dee-um ay-KAW-lee)

This rare wildflower is a native orchid. In the Upstate, it's found in mountain forests, often under pine trees, and grows only one flower in the spring with a large pink pouch. Its sweet scent attracts bees, which get trapped inside. With only one exit, the bees are forced to rub pollen on the flower's stigma on the way out, which pollinates the flower.

Where: Mountain parks and wild spaces with pine forests during mid-spring

Quercus (KWER-kus) 🔭
Oak genus

Quercus is the latin name for the oak tree genus. There are several native oaks in the Upstate, and common ones like white, blackjack, and post are called "keystone" because they feed and house hundreds of other species. More than 900 species of butterflies and moths rely on oaks to feed caterpillars, which feed baby birds. Acorns feed squirrels, black bears, wild turkey, and deer. When oak leaves fall in autumn, leave them beneath the tree so caterpillars can rest there over the winter.

Where: Backyards, parks, and wild spaces

Rosebay rhododendron 🔭 🔭
Rhododendron maximum (roh-doh-DEN-dron MAKS-ih-mum)

These wild bushes grow all over the mountains in the Upstate. Their long, oval leaves are evergreen, which provide shelter in the winter for small birds and mammals, and their strong roots help prevent erosion, which is especially helpful along mountain rivers and streams. Their beautiful pink and white blooms tell us that summer is on its way.

Where: Mountain parks and wild spaces

Swamp rabbit 🔭 🔭 🔭
Sylvilagus aquaticus (sil-vih-LAY-gus uh-KWAH-tih-kus)

The swamp rabbit, the largest rabbit in South Carolina, is a rare find. It lives in the western part of the Upstate in dense thickets near swamps, lakes, and rivers. It has rusty brown fur and eats grasses and sedges. The swamp rabbit is considered an imperiled species because much of its habitat has been lost due to river damming and land clearing for development.

Where: Parks and wild spaces with dense thickets near wetlands

Turtle, eastern painted 🔭
Chrysemys picta (kry-SEE-mis PIK-tuh)

This small turtle is called painted for the telltale yellow or red stripes on its legs and outer shell. It likes to bask in the sun on logs in large groups and snacks on plants, fish, and bugs. During the winter, it buries under the mud floors of ponds and lakes to brumate. It uses special blood vessels under its tail to absorb oxygen and can stay there for more than 100 days.

Where: Backyards, parks, and wild spaces with water

Ursus americanus (UR-sus ah-mer-ih-KAY-nus) 🔭 🔭 🔭
American black bear

The American black bear is the only bear in our state, but it isn't always black. Sometimes it's brown! Black bears eat wild berries, roots, insects (even bumblebees), fish, and rodents. They like large forests with plenty of food and den sites. If you meet one, give it plenty of space. Talk normally, stand tall, and slowly wave your arms. Walk away backwards at an angle. That way, you can keep your eye on the bear and make sure you're not blocking its only way out.

Where: Spacious mountain parks and wild spaces

Viburnum, arrowwood 🔭 🔭
Viburnum dentatum (vy-BUR-num den-TAY-tum)

There are several types of this native shrub, but *Viburnum dentatum*, or arrowwood, is a great food source for bees, butterflies, and birds. Clusters of small white flowers bloom in spring and change into blue-black berries during late summer—a real treat for songbirds! Native people used the straight stems of this shrub for arrows, hence the name "arrowwood."

Where: Parks and wild spaces with wet woodlands

Witches' butter 👓
Tremella mesenterica (treh-MEL-uh mes-en-TER-ih-kuh)

This jelly fungus is common across the world, but it especially likes warm, wet places with plenty of dead logs. As a fungi, witches' butter isn't a plant or animal. It's a parasite that feeds on other parasites that eat dead trees. The name comes from an old myth that if it grew on your doorframe, it was a sign of a witch's spell. Boil it with sugar, then dry it out to make candy.

Where: Backyards, parks, and wild spaces with dead wood

Xylocopa virginica (ZY-loh-KOH-puh ver-JIN-ih-kuh) 👓
Eastern carpenter bee

The carpenter bee is similar in size to a bumblebee, but it's less fuzzy and has a full black abdomen instead of yellow stripes. The female bee burrows into wood to build a nest, and while she *can* sting, she rarely does. These big native bees are great at pollinating plants, but too many of their holes can cause damage to wooden structures. Build them a wooden bee home to keep them away from fences and decks.

Where: Backyards, parks, and wild spaces with dried wood

Yellow-bellied sapsucker 👓 👓
Sphyrapicus varius (sfy-ruh-PIH-kus VAR-ee-us)

While yellow-bellied sapsuckers can be hard to spot, it's easy to know if they've been around. To get at sap and insects inside trees, they drill a straight row of small holes around tree trunks. Find them in the Upstate from fall to early spring. They live in young woodland forests with maple and birch trees. Their sapwells are also used by ruby-throated hummingbirds.

Where: Wooded areas in backyards and parks during fall through spring

Zebra swallowtail butterfly 👓 👓
Eurytides marcellus (yoo-RIH-tih-deez mar-SEL-us)

These striped butterflies are rarely found away from pawpaw trees, which grow in our forests as understory trees with oval-shaped fruits in late summer. Female swallowtails lay their eggs on pawpaw leaves, which the caterpillars eat when they hatch. If you spot adults grouping in puddles, they are actually getting moisture and minerals from the mud, which is called "puddling."

Where: Backyards, parks, and wild spaces with pawpaw trees

FURTHER READING

Explore the following resources with an adult to help identify different species and learn more about native wildlife.

Apps

eBird

iNaturalist

iPhone Photos

Merlin

PictureThis

Seek

Organizations

Conestee Nature Preserve
conesteepreserve.org

Roper Mountain Science Center
ropermountain.org

South Carolina Botanical Garden
clemson.edu/scbg

South Carolina Department of Natural Resources
(SC Bat Watch) *dnr.sc.gov*

South Carolina Native Plant Society
scnps.org

South Carolina Natural Heritage Program
heritagetrust.dnr.sc.gov

South Carolina Wildlife Federation
scwf.org

Websites

inaturalist.org

natureserve.org

gcbirdclub.org

ebird.org

kidsinparks.com

homegrownnationalpark.org

namethatplant.net

irma.nps.gov/NPSpecies

Upstate Outdoor Exploration Guide

Discover native wild things in these protected outdoor spaces in South Carolina

Abbeville County
Calhoun Falls State Park / Parsons Mountain Recreation Area

Anderson County
Clemson Experimental Forest / Rocky River Nature Park / Sadlers Creek State Park

Cherokee County
Cowpens National Battlefield / Kings Mountain National Military Park

Greenwood County
Lake Greenwood State Park / Ninety Six National Historic Site

Greenville County
Bunched Arrowhead Heritage Preserve / Conestee Nature Preserve / Mountain Bridge Wilderness Area (Jones Gap & Caesars Head State Parks) / Paris Mountain State Park / Roper Mountain Science Center

Laurens County
Battle of Musgrove Mill State Historic Site / Joe R. Adair Outdoor Education Center

Oconee County
Andrew Pickens Ranger District, Sumter National Forest / Clemson Experimental Forest / Devils Fork State Park / Jocassee Gorges Wildlife Management Area / Lake Hartwell State Park / Oconee State Park / Oconee Station State Historic Site

Pickens County
Clemson Experimental Forest / Eastatoe Creek Heritage Preserve / Keowee-Toxaway State Park / Nalley Brown Nature Park / Nine Times Preserve / South Carolina Botanical Garden / Table Rock State Park

Spartanburg County
Croft State Park / Hatcher Garden / Pacolet River Heritage Preserve

Union County
Enoree Ranger District, Sumter National Forest / Rose Hill Plantation State Historic Site

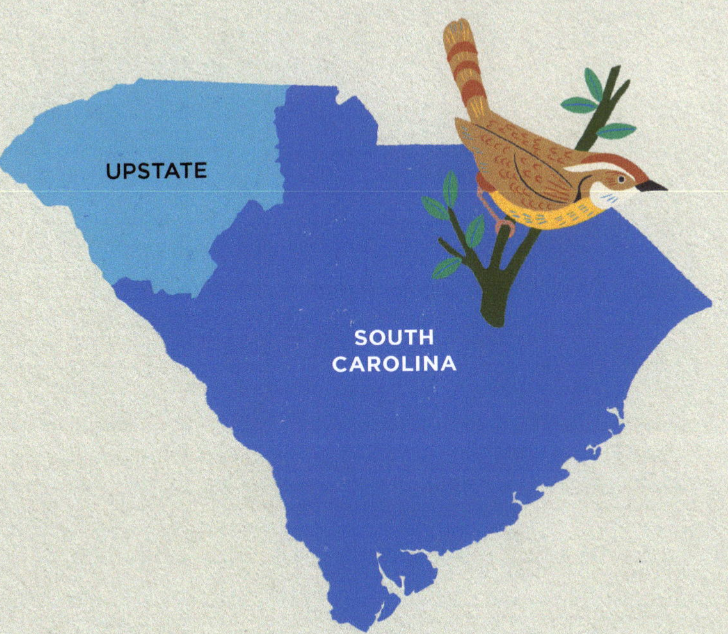

For a complete list of South Carolina heritage preserves and wildlife management areas, visit the South Carolina Department of Natural Resources page online.

MEET THE WILD THINGS TEAM

Abby Moore Keith is a writer based in the Blue Ridge foothills of South Carolina. She spends a lot of time exploring her own backyard and more with her husband Sam, beloved children, and dog named Gus. Her love for the natural world and the creatures that call it home inspires her work.
abbymoorekeith.com

Carissa Grace Bowser has been creating art as long as she can remember. With a BA in Studio Art, she and her fellow artist husband run Victory Garden Studio. Over the years they have collaborated on many projects from murals and children's book illustrations to posters and prints. She also finds inspiration in the nearby Blue Ridge Mountains. She does her best to spend time outside taking in the beauty of the trails, lakes, and waterfalls nearby.
victorygardenstudio.com

Lib Ramos is the designer and founder of Good Printed Things, an independent publishing company. She loves projects that facilitate collaboration between writers, designers, and artists. She is passionate about print design and exploring the role that physical objects play in our increasingly digital world.
goodprintedthings.com

www.ingramcontent.com/pod-product-compliance
Lightning Source LLC
Chambersburg PA
CBHW042204030726
47602CB00008B/126